For my grandchildren, Lucas, Lauren, and Colin – Patrick

To Mark and Greta, Mom and Dad – Anne

First Edition 2010
Kane Miller, A Division of EDC Publishing

Text copyright © Patrick Young, 1993
Illustrations copyright © Anne Lee, 2010

For information contact:
Kane Miller, A Division of EDC Publishing
PO Box 470663
Tulsa, OK 74147-0663
www.kanemiller.com
www.edcpub.com

Library of Congress Control Number: 2009934751

Manufactured by Regent Publishing Services, Hong Kong
Printed May 2010 in ShenZhen, Guangdong, China
1 2 3 4 5 6 7 8 9 10

ISBN: 978-1-935279-23-5

OLD ABE, EAGLE HERO

The Civil War's Most Famous Mascot

Written by Patrick Young
Illustrated by Anne Lee

Kane Miller
A DIVISION OF EDC PUBLISHING

Up in the Northwoods of Wisconsin, many years ago, there lived an American Indian man named Chief Sky.

One day in 1861, Chief Sky found a baby Bald Eagle in a nest high in a tree. The tiny eagle was no bigger than a man's fist.

Chief Sky carried the little bird to his village, where the women and children fed and cared for the eaglet.

When Chief Sky's people paddled down the river to sell their furs, they took the young eagle with them and traded him to a farmer named Dan McCann.

The eagle went to live with the McCann family. Sometimes at night, Farmer McCann played the fiddle, and the eagle would hop up and down in time to the music.

Many of Farmer McCann's neighbors left their farms to fight in the Civil War on the side of the North.

But Farmer McCann could not fight because he had a bad leg, so he sent his eagle to war in his place.

The eagle joined a company of Wisconsin soldiers. They called their new mascot "Old Abe," in honor of President Abraham Lincoln.

The soldiers made a wooden perch for Old Abe and trimmed it with tiny American flags. They carried Old Abe in the front rank as they marched away to battle.

By the time Old Abe went to war he was almost fully grown.

He was as tall as a two-year-old child, but weighed only about eight pounds. When he spread his wings, they measured nearly seven feet from tip to tip.

Old Abe was very brave in battle.

He jumped up and down on his perch and screamed at the enemy.

He did not seem afraid of the bullets that whizzed past him.

The enemy soldiers from the South hated Old Abe. They knew that his courage made the Northern soldiers fight harder.

At Corinth, Mississippi, a Southern general ordered his men to capture Old Abe. Twice the Southern soldiers charged. Twice the Northern soldiers pushed them back. Old Abe spread his wings wide as the enemy charged a third time.

Suddenly, a bullet grazed one of Old Abe's wings, and another cut the cord that tied him to his perch. Old Abe flew into the air.

For a moment, he hovered over the battlefield. Then he flew behind the Northern lines to safety. One of his friends rushed to him, but Old Abe was not badly hurt.

This battle made Old Abe famous. Newspapers printed long stories about him, and people in the North loved to talk about "The Eagle Hero," and his adventures.

When the soldiers camped after a battle, Old Abe relaxed. He fished for minnows in the rivers and played tricks on his friends. Sometimes he tipped over their water buckets. Sometimes he tore their clothes. And sometimes he took their food.

But the soldiers loved Old Abe. They taught him to shake hands and to drink water from a canteen.

Old Abe took part in the famous battle at Vicksburg, Mississippi, in 1863. Cannons roared, and shells exploded as the Northern Army charged.

The soldier who was carrying Old Abe stumbled and fell, and a Southern bullet tore a few feathers from Old Abe's neck. But the eagle sprang from his perch and dragged his buddy to safety.

Later, a cannon ball landed near Old Abe and another soldier. The blast smashed the canteen the soldier was holding, but he and Old Abe escaped harm.

The soldiers thought Old Abe was their lucky charm, and many of them wanted to carry his perch. During the war, six different soldiers carried Old Abe, and none of them was ever hurt while holding the eagle.

The original members of Old Abe's company once took him home with them on leave. When they returned, some of the other soldiers were surprised. Old Abe's head feathers had turned white. (Eagles like Old Abe are called Bald Eagles because their white heads look bald from a distance.)

Old Abe helped his soldier friends capture a Southern camp one night. As the soldiers crept near the enemy, Old Abe whistled. He was warning his friends that a stranger was close by. The stranger was a Southern soldier, and Abe's friends captured him. They made their captive tell them the password to the Southern outpost.

Once they knew the password, it was easy for the Northern soldiers to sneak into the Southern camp and capture it. Old Abe was with them, screaming his victory cry.

Old Abe saw his last battle in 1864. He had fought bravely in twenty-five major battles and many more minor clashes. His soldier friends sent him home to safety. They voted to give him to their state. Old Abe went to live in the Wisconsin Capitol Building. He had a two-room apartment with a bird bath built just for him. And in nice weather, Old Abe played on the Capitol's lawn with his keeper. People came from all over the country to see Old Abe in his new home.

In 1865, Old Abe took part in a big fair in Chicago. People paid five dollars each for his old feathers. P.T. Barnum, the famous showman and circus owner, wanted to buy Old Abe for $20,000 – but Wisconsin refused to sell its hero.

Old Abe lived for many years. He remembered his soldier friends who carried him in battle when they came to see him. He would spread his wings in welcome, rub the cheek of his old friend and coo.

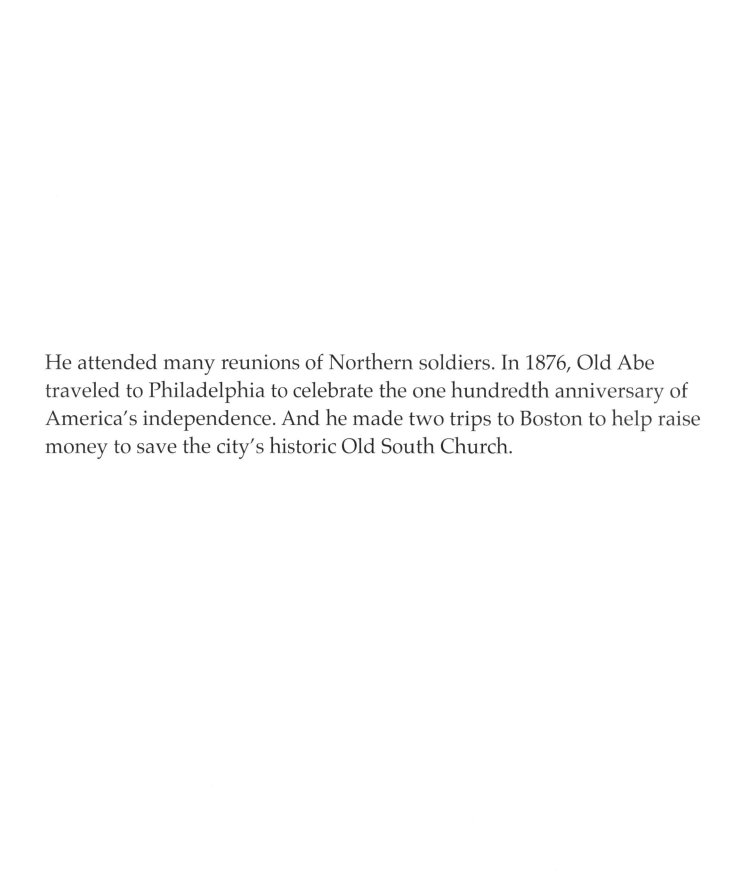

He attended many reunions of Northern soldiers. In 1876, Old Abe traveled to Philadelphia to celebrate the one hundredth anniversary of America's independence. And he made two trips to Boston to help raise money to save the city's historic Old South Church.

Fifty-nine species of eagles live throughout the world, except in icy Antarctica. Bald Eagles live only in North America.

Eagles have stood for strength and courage for more than 2,500 years. Soldiers of ancient Persia and Rome carried eagles into battle, as Old Abe's friends did. American Indians received eagle feathers for their bravery.

Congress selected the Bald Eagle as the U.S. national emblem in 1789. It did so over the protests of Benjamin Franklin. He wanted the Wild Turkey as the country's national bird. The Bald Eagle appears on the Great Seal of the United States. You will also find it on the President's flag and on some coins and paper money.

Bald Eagles live all over the United States – except for in Hawaii – and in Canada and northern Mexico. They build their nests in tall trees or on high cliffs near water. Their favorite food is fish, which they catch in lakes and streams.

The birds mate for life. The mother lays two or three eggs each year. The eggs hatch in about thirty-five days. Three months later, the young birds can fly and hunt for themselves. Old Abe lived for twenty years. Some Bald Eagles live up to thirty years.

Two U.S. laws protect Bald Eagles from hunters and other dangers. They outlaw killing, harassing and other actions that harm the large birds.

However, the Bald Eagle's greatest threat came from DDT. This insecticide was used to kill mosquitoes and other pests. DDT washed into lakes and rivers. It contaminated the fish living there. When Bald Eagles ate the fish, the DDT weakened the shells of their eggs. The shells cracked before the baby eagles could hatch.

In the early 1960s, the number of Bald Eagle pairs fell to less than five hundred in the United States. People feared all the Bald Eagles would die. But the U.S. Government banned the use of DDT. And the Bald Eagle population rebounded.

The country's living symbol is growing larger in numbers. Today, there are more than 6,000 eagle pairs in the United States.